I AM
Discovering Who I Am

A Self-Discovery & Confidence Book for Young Learners

Dr. Tache' Vereen

ISBN: 979-8-9993418-4-6

Published by DOC with TV LLC

Book Cover & Layout Design: Abu Bakar Javed

TABLE OF CONTENTS

Your Adventure Starts Here!

Hello, friend!

This is no ordinary book. It's a special book to help you see just how amazing you are. You are special—just the way you are!

No matter what you are going through, always remember that you are strong and capable.

Take your time as you go through this book. If you have questions, it's okay to ask a parent, teacher, or someone you trust for help. There is nothing wrong with asking for help!

Most of all, have fun and enjoy this journey as you discover more about YOU!

CHAPTER 1

A Moment in Gym Class

When I was in elementary school, I loved to learn.

One day in gym class, everyone was running and playing indoor hockey.

Shoes squeaked.

Hockey sticks tapped.

The puck slid across the floor.

My friends laughed and had fun.

And there I was… sitting at the other end of the gym with a book in my hands.

I wasn't trying to skip class.

I just wanted to read.

I felt happy sitting quietly and learning new things.

My book was about how things are made.

I started thinking,

"Maybe I can make something too!

Maybe I can make my own paper one day.

Maybe I can share it.

Maybe I can even sell it!"

No one asked what I was reading.

No one really noticed me.

But I noticed something...

I liked what I was doing.

I liked my ideas.

I didn't need everyone to see me.

I could see myself.

And I knew my ideas mattered.

AMAZING INVENTIONS
SCIENCE
IDEA

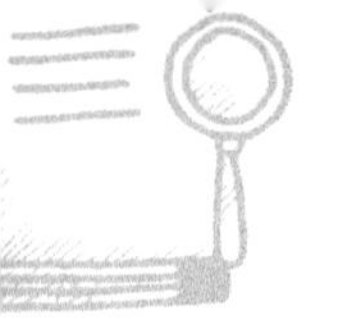

What is something you like to do, even when no one is watching?

____

____

____

____

____

____

____

____

____

Draw something you like to do all by yourself!

Pick words that describe YOU!

curious	confident
creative	thoughtful
focused	smart
independent	brave
imaginative	proud

Say it loud, Say it proud!

I AM___________________________

____

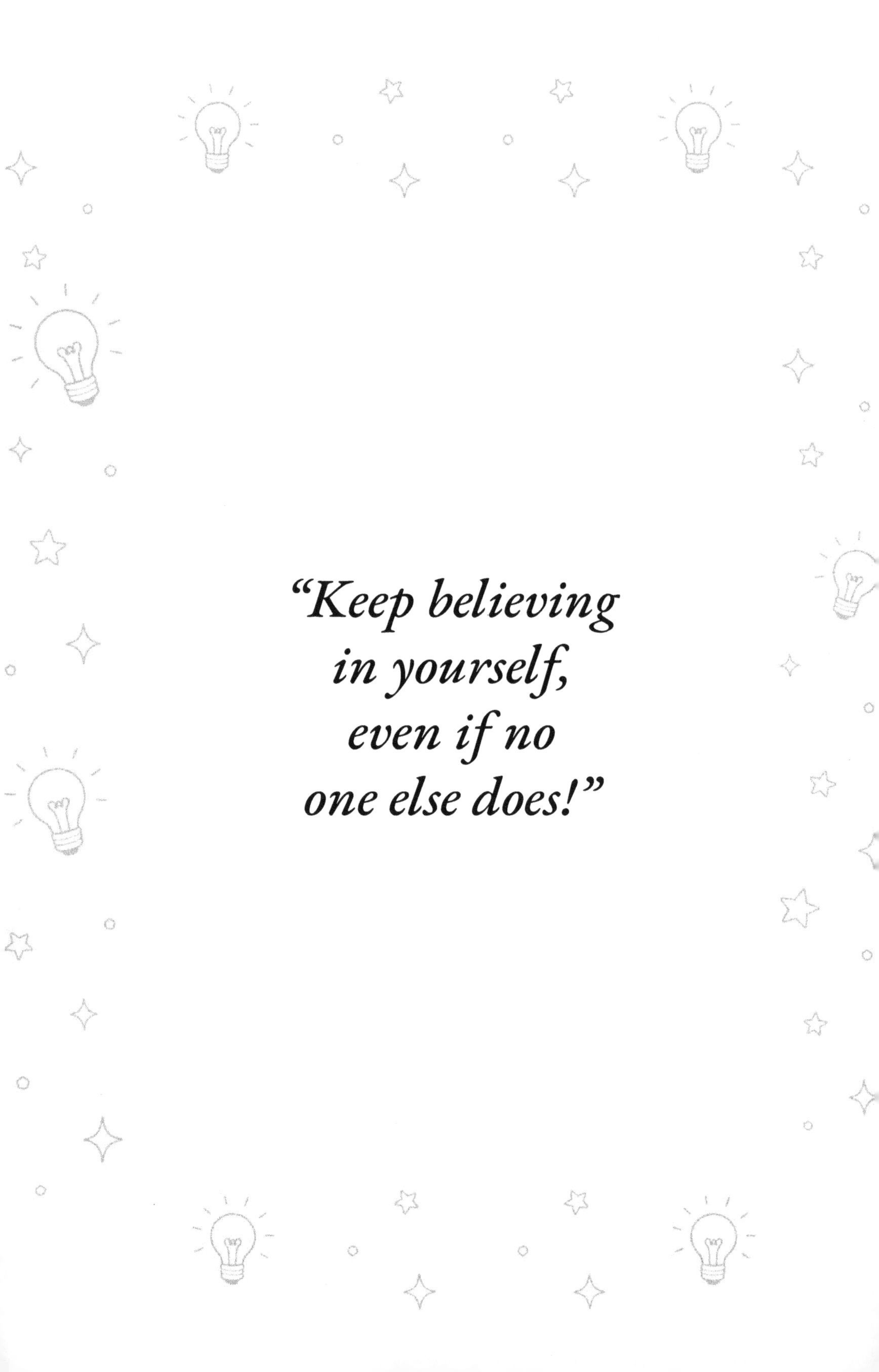

*"Keep believing
in yourself,
even if no
one else does!"*

CHAPTER 2

Words That Stick

One day, my mom took me to the hair salon.

My hair needed fixing because I hadn't taken care of it.

The hairdresser had to cut my hair very short.

When I went to school the next day, some kids called me "bald-headed," and everyone laughed.

I laughed too, but inside I felt hurt.

Their words stayed with me.

Words can make people feel sad.

Later, I remembered a boy at school who wore the same sneakers every day.

Some kids laughed at his shoes.

One day, I laughed too.

But when I saw him walk away with his head down, it made me feel sad.

That's when I learned something important.

Words can hurt people.

But words can also help people feel strong and happy.

So I try to use my words to be kind.

I try to speak words that make someone smile.

HURTFUL WORDS
KIND WORDS
Be
espectful
Choos
Kindne

Have words ever made you feel sad? What happened?

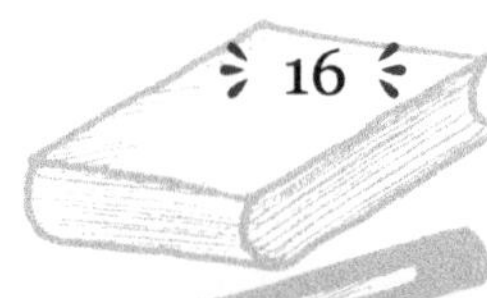

Draw someone using kind words to make a friend smile.

Pick words that describe YOU!

kind	friendly
caring	encouraging
gentle	nice
respectful	thoughtful
helpful	loving

Say it loud, Say it proud!

I AM

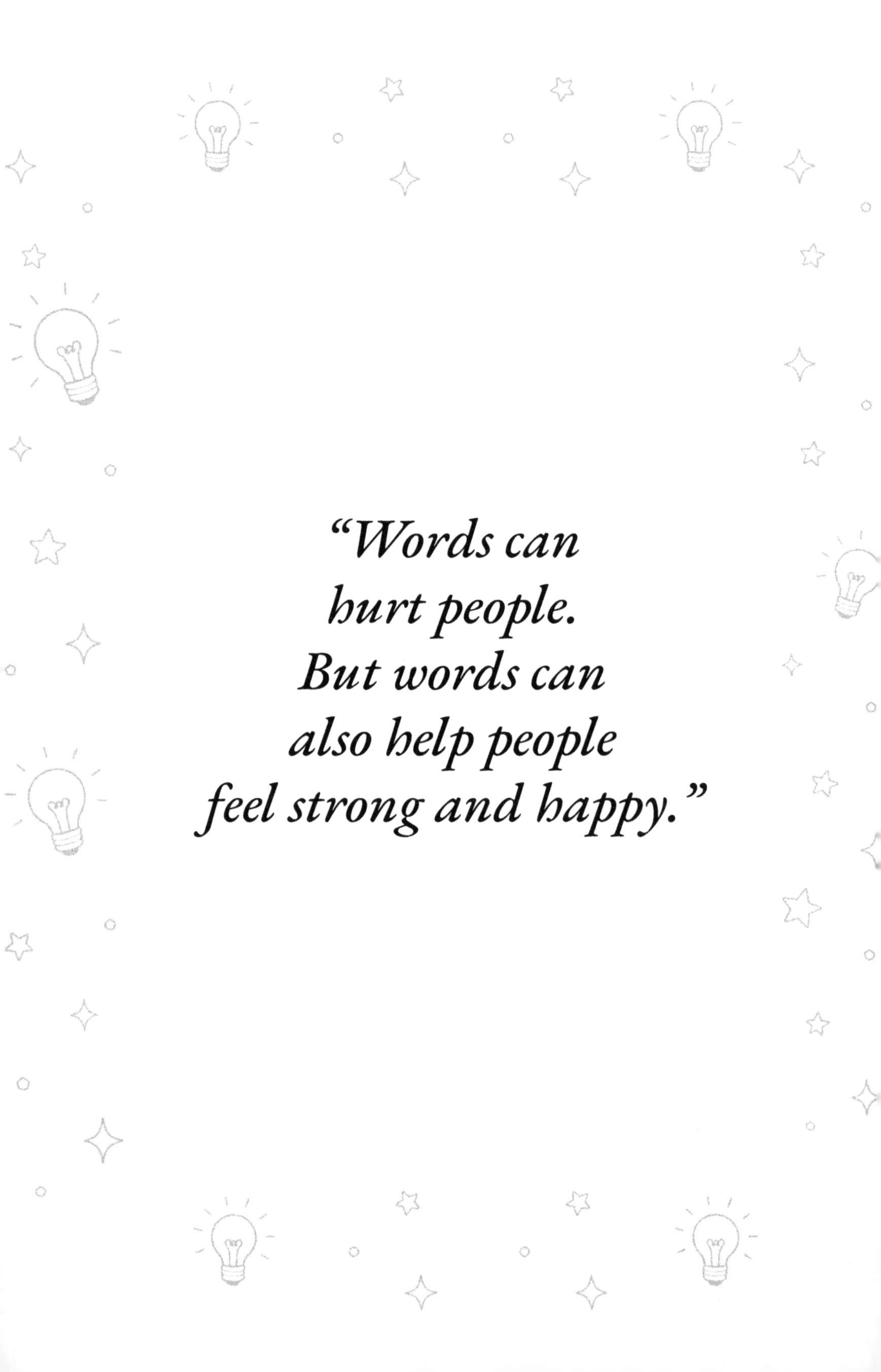

"Words can
hurt people.
But words can
also help people
feel strong and happy."

CHAPTER 3

I Watch and I Learn

When I was little, I had a neighbor who was like a grandfather to all the kids on our street.

Every time he saw us, he would stop, smile, and talk.

He told stories, but even more, he listened to everything we said.

He was patient. He never rushed us.

He answered all our questions—even the silly ones.

That made us feel special.

Sometimes he invited us to church.

He even helped our parents give us a ride.

Watching him care for us made me feel special.

I noticed something important: kids are always watching the people around them.

We learn from how they act, how they speak, and how they treat others.

Even small things, like helping a friend or waiting his turn, taught me how to be kind, patient, and caring.

Sometimes we might see someone make a wrong choice.

They might not be kind or might not listen.

When that happens, we can choose to do the right thing.

We can choose to be kind.

We can choose to be patient.

We can choose to do the right thing—even when others do not.

Next time you see someone being kind, or helping others, notice it.

You are learning every day.

I learn by
watching
kindness
in action

What kind thing can you do today?

Draw something you can do to make someone smile.

Pick words that describe YOU!

patient	helpful
kind	caring
polite	gentle
respectful	fair
honest	responsible

____

____

____

____

____

Say it loud, Say it proud!

I AM______________________________

____

____

____

____

____

____

"We can
choose to be kind."

CHAPTER 4

The People Who Show Up

When I was a little older, I loved spending time with my friends.

We would go to the mall, walk around, and laugh together.

But my mom started to notice something.

She saw that I was paying a lot of attention to boys.

My mom cared about me and wanted to help me make good choices.

So she did something special.

She called some of my older cousins and my aunt.

They all came together and sat with me.

One by one, they talked to me.

They told me they cared about me.

They wanted me to focus and do my best.

At first, I thought they were telling me what to do.

Then I listened.

I heard kind words.

I saw caring hearts.

I felt their love.

They were not trying to control me.

They were trying to help me.

That day, I learned something important.

People who love you will show up for you.

They may talk to you.

They may guide you.

They may help you make good choices.

Sometimes it may not feel good at first.

But that is because they care about you.

We all need people who show up for us.

And one day, you can show up for someone too.

Who has helped you?
How did it make you feel?

Draw a way
you can help someone.

Pick words that describe YOU!

loved

supported

safe

thankful

grateful

cared for

important

valued

strong

connected

Say it loud, Say it proud!

I AM _______________________________

____

____

____

____

____

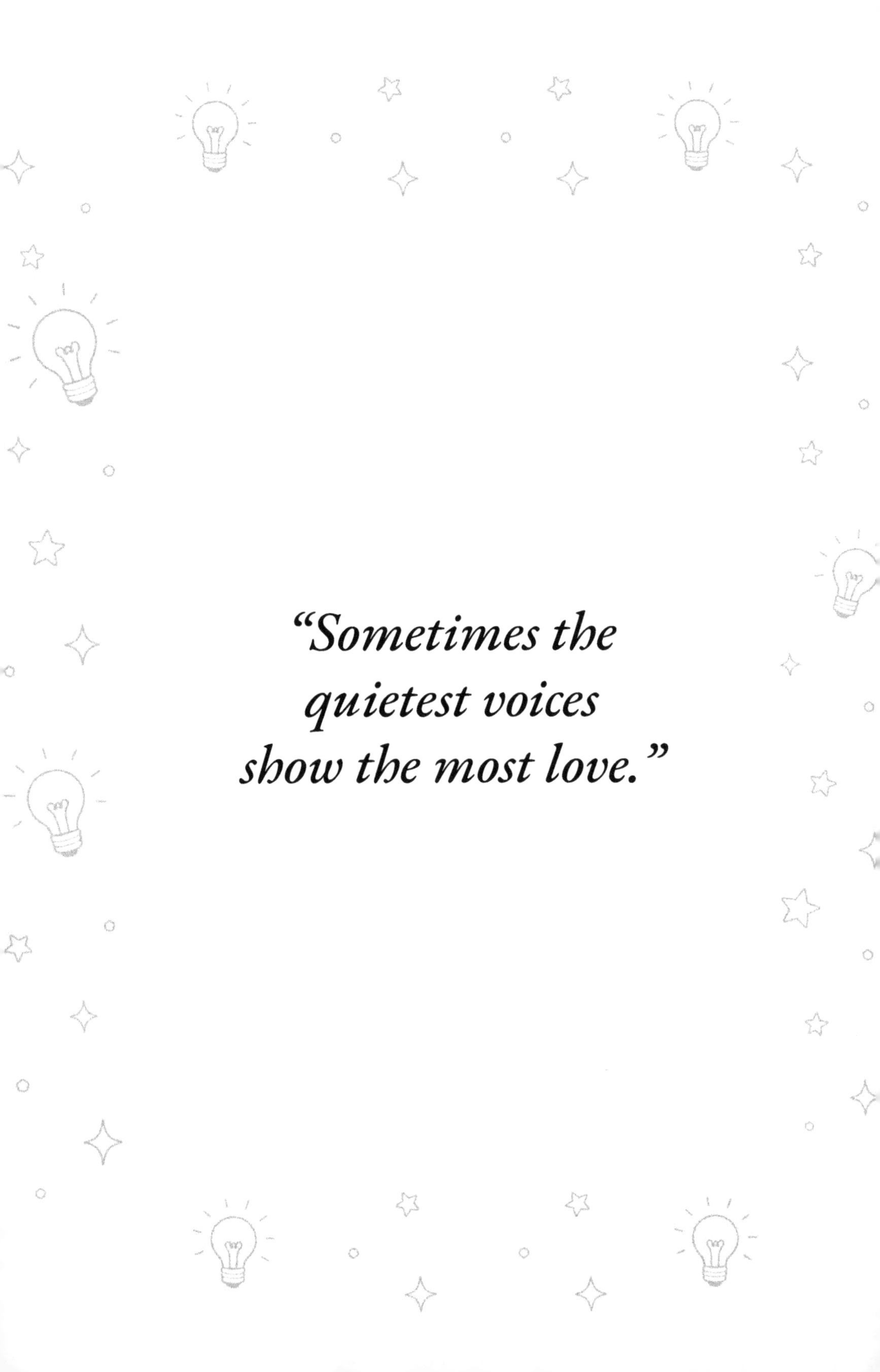

"Sometimes the
quietest voices
show the most love."

CHAPTER 5

Being Uniquely You

When I was little, I was very skinny.

Some kids called me "sticks and bones."

That made me feel sad. I didn't understand why they laughed.

I just wanted to fit in.

Sometimes I wore extra clothes to look bigger.

It was cold, but it made running and playing hard.

I tried to eat more, but my body didn't change the way I wanted.

My mom told me I was beautiful.

She said I could be a model. That made me feel happy and special.

She even took me to modeling events so I could try new things.

I loved reading books and making things.

Some friends noticed and asked me about what I was doing.

They thought it was amazing. I felt proud.

One day, I made my own paper and sold it to my friends.

They were amazed! I felt proud of myself.

I learned that being me is enough.

Everyone is different. Everyone has special talents.

Maybe you are a good runner, a good friend, or a good listener. That makes you special.

Celebrate what makes you special.

Celebrate the differences in others too.

You don't have to be like anyone else.

Be yourself, because being you is the best!

I AM UNIQUE.
I AM ENOUGH.
This is ME!
CREATIVE
TALENTED
STRONG
SMART
MY GIFT
MY STORY
MY PURPOSE
BEING MYSELF IS MY SUPERPOWER!
I AM ME
7

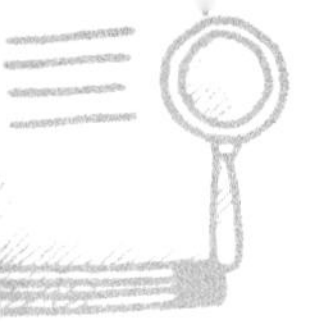

What makes you special?

Draw something
that makes you special!

Pick words that describe YOU!

special   happy

unique   proud

confident   different

brave   kind

strong   amazing

Say it loud, Say it proud!

I AM _______________________

____

____

____

____

____

____

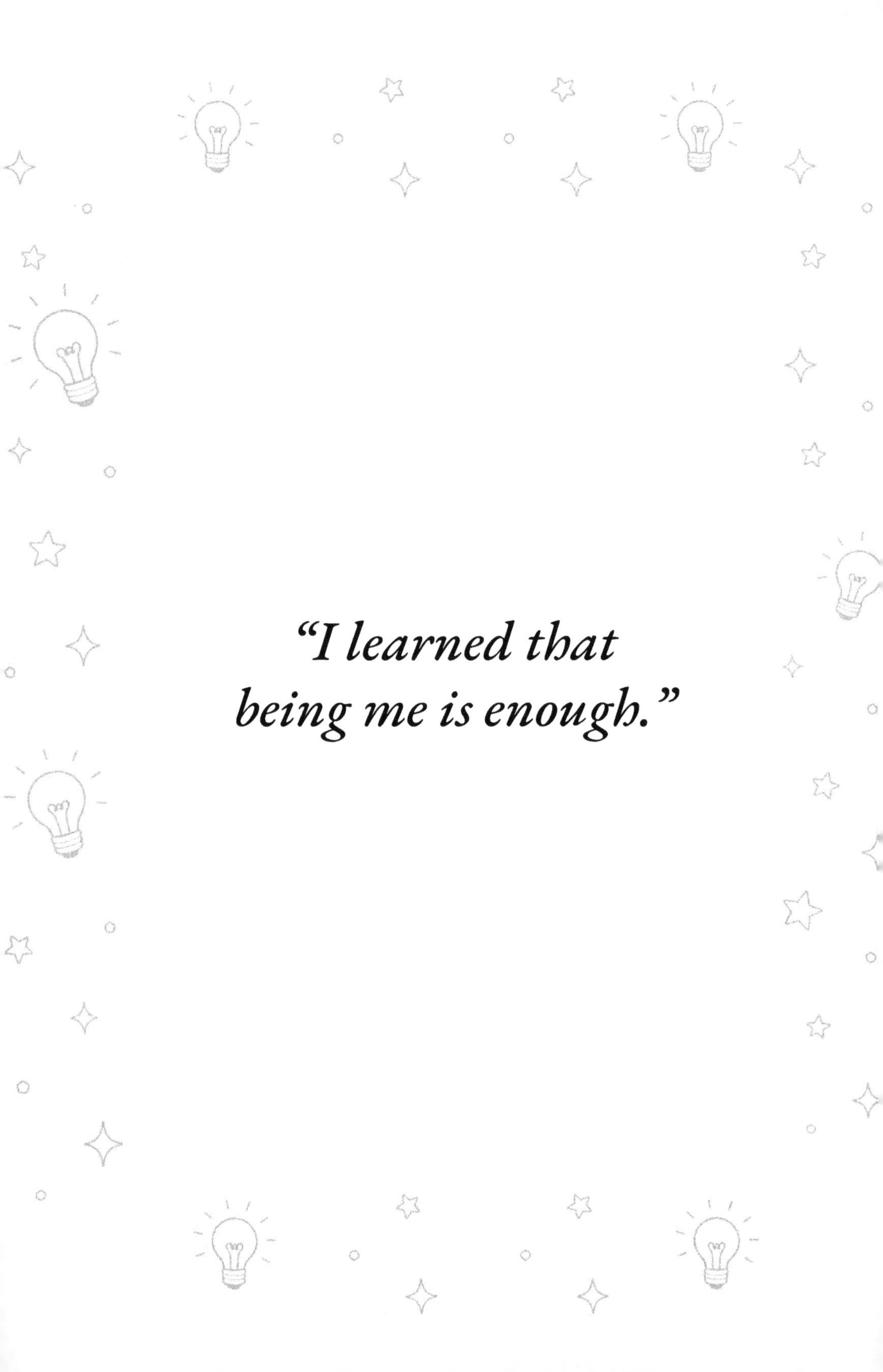

"I learned that
being me is enough."

My
I AM
Declaration

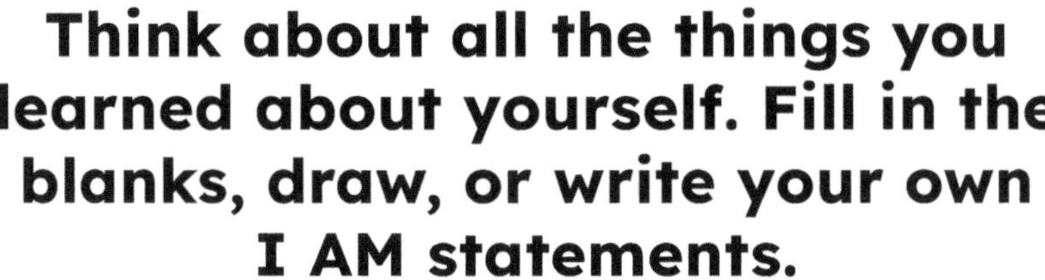

Think about all the things you learned about yourself. Fill in the blanks, draw, or write your own I AM statements.

Say it loud, Say it proud!

____

____

____

____

____

Extra Journal and Doodle Pages

Your Extra Journal & Doodle Pages. Keep Exploring You! Draw, Write, and Celebrate!

Your Extra Journal & Doodle Pages. Keep Exploring You! Draw, Write, and Celebrate!

Your Extra Journal & Doodle Pages. Keep Exploring You! Draw, Write, and Celebrate!

Your Extra Journal & Doodle Pages. Keep Exploring You! Draw, Write, and Celebrate!

Your Extra Journal & Doodle Pages. Keep Exploring You! Draw, Write, and Celebrate!

Your Extra Journal & Doodle Pages. Keep Exploring You! Draw, Write, and Celebrate!

Your Extra Journal & Doodle Pages. Keep Exploring You! Draw, Write, and Celebrate!

Your Extra Journal & Doodle Pages. Keep Exploring You! Draw, Write, and Celebrate!

Your Extra Journal & Doodle Pages. Keep Exploring You! Draw, Write, and Celebrate!

Your Extra Journal & Doodle Pages. Keep Exploring You! Draw, Write, and Celebrate!

Your Extra Journal & Doodle Pages. Keep Exploring You! Draw, Write, and Celebrate!

A Final Message to You

You Did It! Look at You!

I hope you discovered something amazing about yourself!

 You should be proud.

Now, remember what you learned about you and keep noticing the good in yourself and the people around you.

If you ever need a reminder, look back at what you wrote or drew—you'll see just how special you are!

Guide for Parents and Teachers

Welcome

This book is designed to help children explore feelings, self-awareness, and kindness. The stories, reflection questions, doodle pages, and I AM declarations are most powerful when shared with an adult. Use this guide to support discussion, guide reflection, and celebrate your child's growth.

Reading Together

- Read one chapter at a time and pause to discuss the story.

- Ask your child the reflection questions aloud.

- Encourage them to share their thoughts, feelings, or experiences.

- Let them take their time with the doodle, journal, and I AM pages.

Reflection & Journaling

- Use the journal and doodle pages to explore emotions and ideas.

- Celebrate all responses, even small or simple answers.

- Encourage your child to say their statements out loud.

- Ask them to explain their words or draw examples.

- Reinforce positivity: "I love how you are being kind!" or "You are proud of yourself — that's wonderful!"

- Use the final Big I AM declaration page to summarize all the child's strengths and accomplishments.

Talking About Each Chapter

Chapter 1   **A Moment in Gym Class:** Talk about self-confidence, curiosity, and celebrating personal interests.

Chapter 2   **Words That Stick:** Discuss the power of words and how to use them kindly.

Chapter 3   **I Watch and I Learn:** Explore learning from others' actions and making good choices.

Chapter 4   **The People Who Show Up:** Highlight gratitude and appreciation for supportive adults and friends.

Chapter 5   **Being Uniquely You!:** Encourage self-acceptance and celebrate uniqueness.

For Adults

- Model the behaviors you want to reinforce — kindness, patience, and respect.

- Encourage your child to notice positive behaviors in friends, siblings, and classmates.

- Celebrate achievements, no matter how small, and reinforce I AM statements daily.

- Adapt discussions to your child's age, personality, and experiences.

About the Author

Dr. Tache' Vereen is an author, speaker, and coach dedicated to helping individuals discover who they are, take ownership of their choices, and cultivate meaningful growth. As the founder of DOC with TV LLC and creator of The DOC Coaching Method™, she is passionate about empowering the next generation to walk confidently in their identity and purpose.